Harry Potter AND THE CHAMBER OF SECRETS

This instrumental series is arranged for Flute, Trumpet, Clarinet, Alto Sax, Tenor Sax, Horn in F, and Trombone. The arrangements are completely compatible with each other and can be played together or as solos. Each book includes a fully orchestrated accompaniment CD. Each song on the CD includes a complete demonstration track, which contains a live performance of the appropriate instrument, followed by a play-along accompaniment track. In addition, an optional piano accompaniment book is available.

Arranged by Bill Galliford, Ethan Neuburg and Tod Edmondson
Project Manager: Carol Cuellar
Art Layout: Michael Ramsay

Album Cover Artwork © 2002 Warner Bros.

WARNER BROS. PUBLICATIONS
Warner Music Group
An AOL Time Warner Company
USA: 15800 NW 48th Avenue, Miami, FL 33014

IMP
INTERNATIONAL MUSIC PUBLICATIONS LIMITED

ENGLAND: GRIFFIN HOUSE,
161 HAMMERSMITH ROAD, LONDON W6 8BS

CONTENTS

	BOOK	CD TRACK	
	PAGE NO.	DEMO	PLAY-ALONG
TUNING NOTE		1	
DOBBY THE HOUSE ELF	9	2	3
THE CHAMBER OF SECRETS	10	4	5
FAWKES THE PHOENIX	12	6	7
MOANING MYRTLE	14	8	9
HARRY'S WONDROUS WORLD	16	10	11
GILDEROY LOCKHART	19	12	13
NIMBUS 2000	20	14	15
FAMILY PORTRAIT	22	16	17
HEDWIG'S THEME	24	18	19

DOBBY THE HOUSE ELF

Music by **JOHN WILLIAMS**

© 2002 WARNER-BARHAM MUSIC, LLC (BMI)
All Rights Administered by WARNER-TAMERLANE PUBLISHING CORP. (BMI)

THE CHAMBER OF SECRETS

Music by **JOHN WILLIAMS**

FAWKES THE PHOENIX

Music by JOHN WILLIAMS

*An easier 8th-note alternative figure has been provided.

MOANING MYRTLE

Music by **JOHN WILLIAMS**

HARRY'S WONDROUS WORLD

Music by **JOHN WILLIAMS**

18

101 **Stately and nobly**
legato

117

GILDEROY LOCKHART

Music by **JOHN WILLIAMS**

IFM0241CD

NIMBUS 2000

Music by **JOHN WILLIAMS**

*An easier 8th-note alternative figure has been provided.

*An easier 8th-note alternative figure has been provided.

FAMILY PORTRAIT

Music by **JOHN WILLIAMS**

Slowly, with expression (♩ = 80)

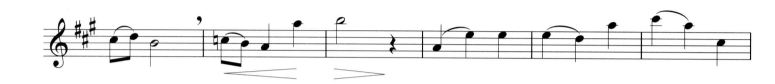

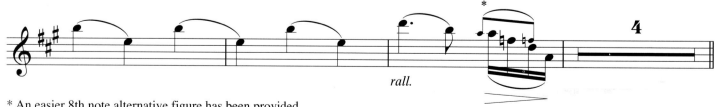

* An easier 8th note alternative figure has been provided.

Family Portrait - 2 - 1
IFM0241CD

HEDWIG'S THEME

Music by **JOHN WILLIAM**

© 2001 WARNER-BARHAM MUSIC, LLC (BMI)
All Rights Administered by WARNER-TAMERLANE PUBLISHING CORP. (BMI)